Countdown
to a
Space Shuttle Launch

Jennifer Dean

CONTENTS

Rigby®

A Harcourt Achieve Imprint

www.Rigby.com
1-800-531-5015

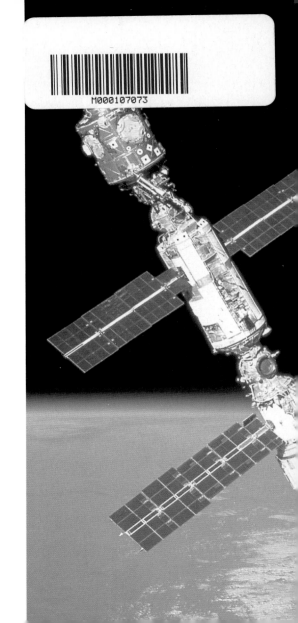

Working on the Space Shuttle Program

All is quiet over the marshy lands of Merritt Island, located between the Indian River and the Banana River on Florida's east coast. Alligators and sea turtles are stirring lazily while birds are already in search of their dinner. Suddenly, a deafening roar shakes the ground as fire and smoke fill the air in a matter of seconds. The birds fly away, noisily protesting the disturbance.

Closer to the action, hundreds of people watch, holding their breath as the space shuttle lifts off from the launch pad. The sight is amazing, even if you have seen it a hundred times before.

Meanwhile, all across the country, people who work on the space shuttle program are watching, too. They're eagerly observing the liftoff from their homes and their jobs, holding their breath along with the rest of the world.

A space shuttle launch is an amazing event to see.

2

USA

People working on the space shuttle program are in many different states across the country, and they each play a role in the success of the launch. Some **engineers** work on the different parts that make up the space shuttle, while others work to find ways to make the space shuttle better. Professional trainers spend hours training the astronauts in everything from diving to conducting experiments. **Nutritionists** make sure that astronauts have a diet that allows them to stay healthy while in space.

NASA Centers Across the United States

Moffett Field, CA
Edwards, CA
Pasadena, CA
Cleveland, OH
Washington, D.C.
Wallops Island, VA
Hampton, VA
Greenbelt, MD
Huntsville, AL
Bay St. Louis, MS
Houston, TX
Cape Canaveral, FL

KEY
= NASA Centers

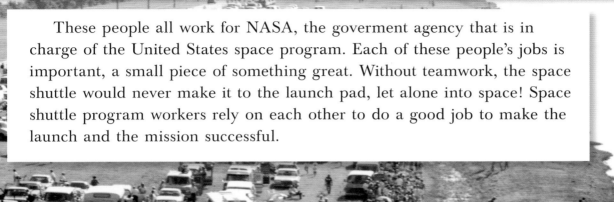

These people all work for NASA, the goverment agency that is in charge of the United States space program. Each of these people's jobs is important, a small piece of something great. Without teamwork, the space shuttle would never make it to the launch pad, let alone into space! Space shuttle program workers rely on each other to do a good job to make the launch and the mission successful.

These people have gathered to watch the shuttle launch.

Mission Planning

Careful planning for a space shuttle mission happens long before the launch pad is reached. Sometimes the planning begins years before a shuttle is even scheduled for liftoff.

Space shuttle mission planners must decide who needs to go on the mission, what must be taken on the shuttle, and what should be done while the shuttle and the astronauts are in space. Making choices about the mission so early can be very hard. In many ways it is like trying to plan a vacation several years before you're supposed to leave.

Imagine if your family tried to plan a vacation the way mission planners must plan for space flights. Not only would you have to decide where to go and what to take with you, but you would have to take all of your own food and supplies. You would have to figure out how to fit everything you needed into your car. If you forgot something, you would have to do without it, because there would be no stores to buy from. You can see how careful planning for a shuttle mission is very important!

These people are busy at work during a space shuttle mission.

So what exactly do astronauts take with them on the shuttle? Besides food and clothes for the astronauts, the shuttle also carries equipment for experiments. If the space shuttle is going to the International Space Station—a huge space laboratory being built by sixteen different countries—the shuttle will carry supplies for the astronauts living there. If something on the Space Station breaks, the shuttle will also carry the tools that are needed to fix it.

International Space Station

When it is completed, the International Space Station will have six labs, where astronauts will conduct experiments ranging from how fire behaves when there is no gravity to observing the effects of pollution on Earth.

The space shuttle is docked at the International Space Station.

Astronaut Training

Being an astronaut isn't just about taking thrilling rides to space, performing weightless somersaults, and eating freeze-dried ice cream! Becoming an astronaut takes an extreme amount of hard work and dedication. Astronauts must complete many hours of training and testing before they even know what mission they will fly on.

Astronauts study the basics of how the space shuttle and the Space Station work. They take tours of all the NASA centers to learn how they work, as well. They also get training in geology, astronomy, and physical fitness.

There are over 2,000 panels, switches, and buttons in the crew cabin, or the area where the astronauts ride. Astronauts must be familiar with all of them.

To learn about these panels, switches, and buttons, the astronauts spend many hours training in shuttle mission **simulators**. These machines are like huge video games that look like the crew cabin of the shuttle.

Training in the simulator allows astronauts to pretend they are on a mission and to practice what they have learned about the space shuttle. Astronauts will spend about three hundred hours in the simulator before the mission ever takes place.

This is what astronauts see in front of them when they fly the space shuttle.

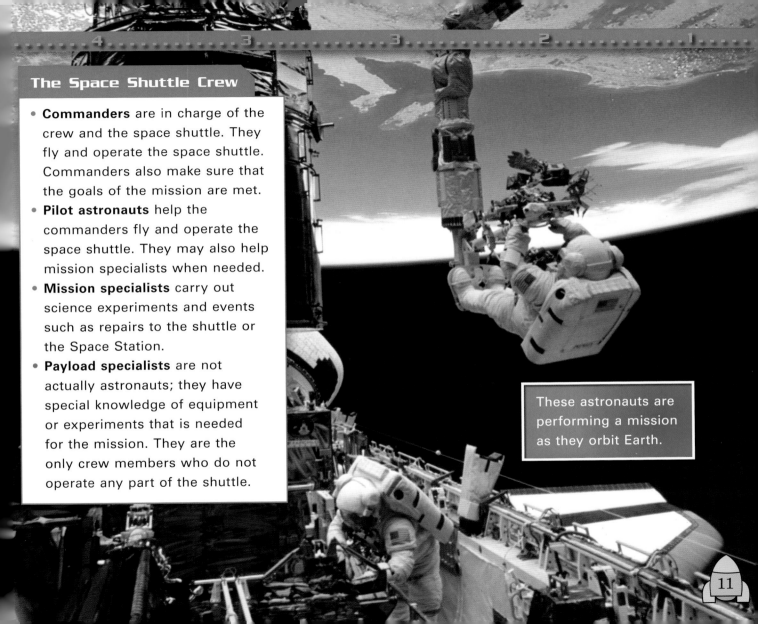

The Space Shuttle Crew

- **Commanders** are in charge of the crew and the space shuttle. They fly and operate the space shuttle. Commanders also make sure that the goals of the mission are met.
- **Pilot astronauts** help the commanders fly and operate the space shuttle. They may also help mission specialists when needed.
- **Mission specialists** carry out science experiments and events such as repairs to the shuttle or the Space Station.
- **Payload specialists** are not actually astronauts; they have special knowledge of equipment or experiments that is needed for the mission. They are the only crew members who do not operate any part of the shuttle.

These astronauts are performing a mission as they orbit Earth.

11

In the neutral **buoyancy** lab, astronauts are given the chance to feel the effects of **weightlessness** before they reach space. This lab is actually a huge swimming pool where the astronauts can train underwater for missions.

Have you ever tried to lift something heavy while under the water? You probably noticed that it is much easier to lift something in the water than it is outside of the water. Things, including our bodies, weigh less in the water, so being underwater can help astronauts feel what it will be like to work with tools in space.

All of this training prepares the astronauts for their mission. It may take a long time for astronauts to learn everything they need to know, but once they do, the mission is usually a success.

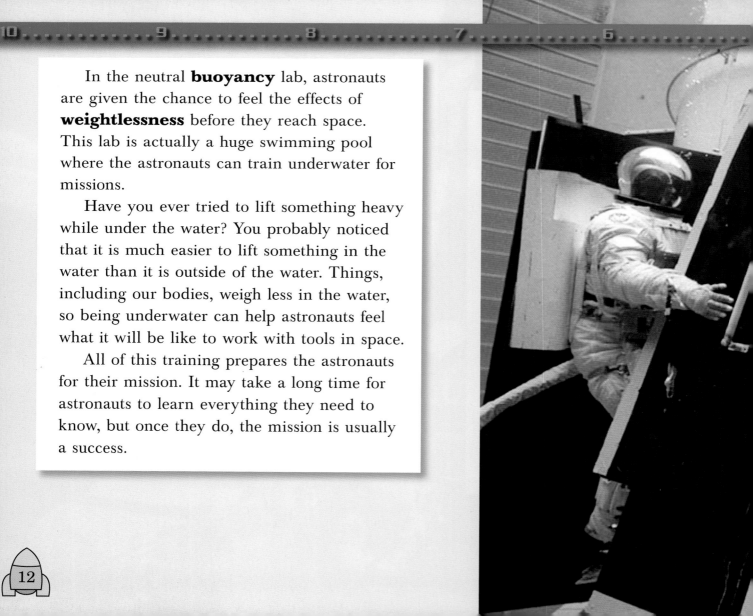

These astronauts are training in the neutral buoyancy lab.

Mission Specialist John L. Phillips

John Phillips is a mission specialist with NASA. He has flown in space twice. Before he became an astronaut, Dr. Phillips studied science, math, and the Russian language in college. He is a scientist who has researched the sun, space, and even NASA spacecraft.

Dr. Phillips was selected to be an astronaut at the age of 45. He has been on two missions, STS-100 on the Space Shuttle *Endeavor*, and Expedition 11 to the International Space Station, where he lived in space for six months and spent almost five hours on a spacewalk outside of the Space Station! In total, Dr. Phillips has spent over 190 days in space.

These are Dr. Phillips' patches from his two missions. Each NASA mission has its own unique patch.

For Expedition 11, he traveled to and from space in the Russian spacecraft *Soyuz*. During this time, the space shuttle was not flying because of the *Columbia* accident. On January 16, 2003, a piece of foam insulation broke off of *Columbia* and hit the shuttle's wing, severely damaging it. NASA and the astronauts were unaware of this, and when the shuttle returned to Earth on February 1, the damage caused *Columbia* to break apart as it attempted to land, tragically killing all seven astronauts on board. Until the cause of the accident was discovered and fixed, NASA was not going to allow a space shuttle to leave Earth.

Astronaut John Phillips, wearing his space suit, is hoping along with his fellow astronauts for a successful mission.

An Interview with John L. Phillips

When you were growing up, did you think you would be an astronaut someday?

I wanted to, but I didn't think I would be able to. But I thought I would have a chance if I just kept trying, and I did. I had to wait a long time to be selected. I spent 20 years applying to be an astronaut, and when I was selected, I was the oldest person ever selected to be an astronaut.

How long did you train for each mission?

I flew on two missions. The first was STS-100, and I trained for about nine months. However, I had trained for several years before that to even be considered. The second mission was the 11th Expedition to the International Space Station, and I trained for about three and a half years for that mission.

John Phillips trained in a buoyancy lab like this one.

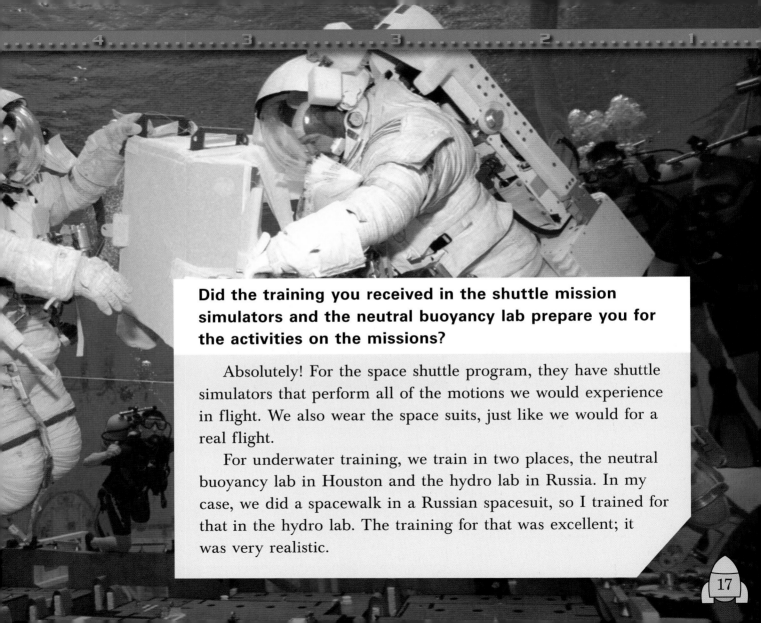

Did the training you received in the shuttle mission simulators and the neutral buoyancy lab prepare you for the activities on the missions?

Absolutely! For the space shuttle program, they have shuttle simulators that perform all of the motions we would experience in flight. We also wear the space suits, just like we would for a real flight.

For underwater training, we train in two places, the neutral buoyancy lab in Houston and the hydro lab in Russia. In my case, we did a spacewalk in a Russian spacesuit, so I trained for that in the hydro lab. The training for that was excellent; it was very realistic.

What were some of your responsibilities during the STS-100 mission?

I was the flight engineer for launch and landing. A flight engineer sits between the pilot and the commander and **monitors** the technical systems of the shuttle and supports the pilot and commander in case of a problem during launch and landing.

During the mission I was also the spacewalk **coordinator**. That means I didn't actually do any spacewalking, but I directed the spacewalk and made sure everything went as planned.

STS-100 flew to the International Space Station, so I was also the person in charge of controlling the **docking** mechanisms on the station. Also, I was a photographer on the mission. I took some of the footage for a movie about the Space Station.

STS-100 Mission Facts

- STS-100 launched into space on April 19, 2001, on the space shuttle *Endeavor*.
- The mission took one piece of a giant robot arm to the International Space Station to help move things around.
- A huge module some people call the "moving van" was also used onboard the shuttle to carry supplies back and forth from the Space Station.

18

You've flown on the Space Shuttle *Endeavor* and the Russian *Soyuz*. How different was it to fly on the Russian spacecraft?

The difference is tremendous! The *Soyuz* capsule is much, much smaller—it is like the space capsules that we had in the 1960s and 1970s—but the space shuttle *Endeavor* is big and roomy and has large wings. The shuttle lands on a runway like an airplane, but the *Soyuz* uses a parachute to land on dry land in the country of Kazakhstan, near Russia.

Astronaut John Phillips and the rest of the crew of STS-100 stand in front of their shuttle.

19

What were your responsibilities aboard the Space Station, and what were some of the science experiments you conducted?

We only have a crew of two on the International Space Station now. Both crew members are responsible for everything. We were both responsible for operating the Russian and American halves of the station. We did one spacewalk in a Russian suit, and we hosted the visit of the shuttle *Discovery*.

Most of the science experiments were about how our bodies and brains responded to the weightless conditions. We also did experiments that measured the activities of the muscles in our lower bodies and the electrical impulses in our brains.

I think of the entire mission as a single experiment. The design of the shuttle, the **payloads**, and the mission control activities are all part of the experiment. And the experiment is ongoing.

You've been a scientist for many years on Earth. How is it different in space?

Well, the main reason it's different is that I'm not designing the experiments anymore; I'm just carrying them out. My job before was to design the experiments. Otherwise, working in a lab on Earth and in space are very similar.

Astronaut John Phillips operates part of the International Space Station.

There's a lot going on during the missions. Did you have much time to sit back and enjoy your time in space?

Well, during the space shuttle flight, I had almost no time. I was busy sixteen hours a day, and then it was time to sleep. On the space shuttle, we all sleep at the same time, so when it's bedtime, people turn out the lights and you have to sleep.

On the International Space Station there are only two crewmembers there for six months at a time, so you can't work at the same pace of a space shuttle mission for that long, so you have more time. I had about three hours a day of personal time, so I spent a lot of that time looking out the window! I read, called, or emailed home, or spent time looking at photos we took and processing them.

Did anything unexpected happen while you were onboard the space shuttle or the Space Station?

No, actually, we were very well trained for everything we had to do up there. There were no big surprises.

Return to Flight

STS-114 was the Return to Flight mission, the first after the space shuttle *Columbia* accident.

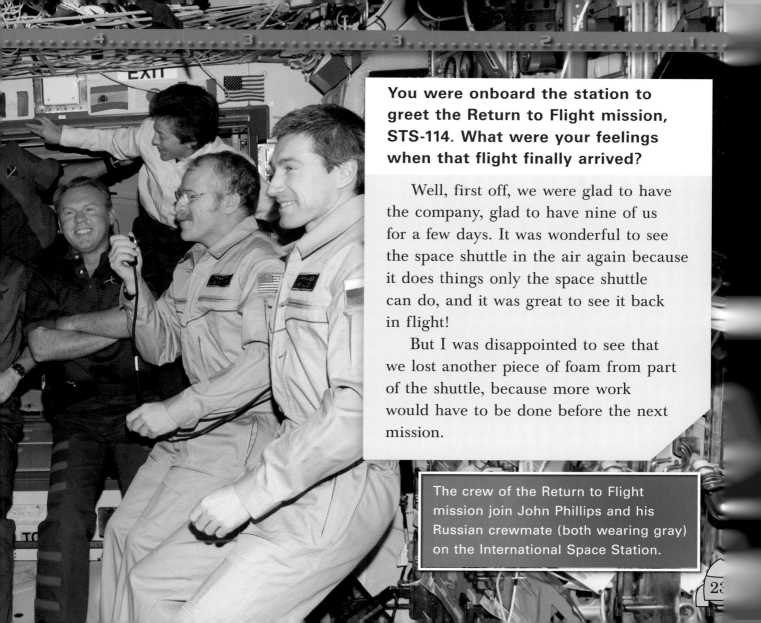

EXIT

You were onboard the station to greet the Return to Flight mission, STS-114. What were your feelings when that flight finally arrived?

Well, first off, we were glad to have the company, glad to have nine of us for a few days. It was wonderful to see the space shuttle in the air again because it does things only the space shuttle can do, and it was great to see it back in flight!

But I was disappointed to see that we lost another piece of foam from part of the shuttle, because more work would have to be done before the next mission.

The crew of the Return to Flight mission join John Phillips and his Russian crewmate (both wearing gray) on the International Space Station.

What was the most exciting part of your time during your second mission, the 11th Expedition to the International Space Station?

The most exciting part I would say was the spacewalk. It was my first. It was really a unique feeling to go outside in the vacuum of space, so it was definitely very, very cool!

How did it feel to set foot on Earth again after spending six months in space? Did your body seem different?

Well, for one thing, it was wonderful to be home. But for the first day or so I was very dizzy, and then for the next few days I felt weak. My muscles weren't used to carrying my weight, but after that I was fine.

Are you ready to fly again?

I am ready to fly again! But right now I'm at the end of the list of the astronauts in line to fly. I'm optimistic I'll get to fly again; it just depends on how things work out!

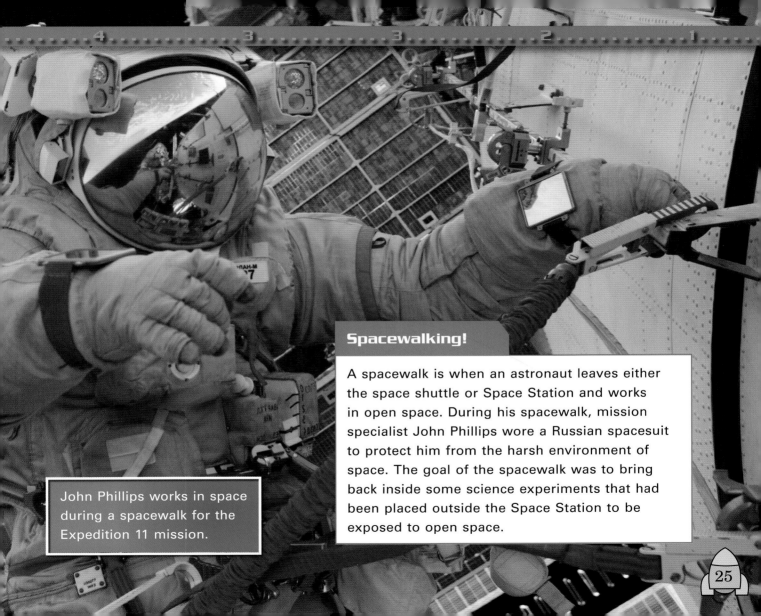

John Phillips works in space during a spacewalk for the Expedition 11 mission.

Spacewalking!

A spacewalk is when an astronaut leaves either the space shuttle or Space Station and works in open space. During his spacewalk, mission specialist John Phillips wore a Russian spacesuit to protect him from the harsh environment of space. The goal of the spacewalk was to bring back inside some science experiments that had been placed outside the Space Station to be exposed to open space.

CHAPTER 5

10 . . . . 9 . . . . 8 . . . . 7 . . . . 6 . . . .

Getting the Shuttle Ready for Launch

The space shuttle is the first spacecraft flown in space that can be reused for more missions. It has more than two and a half million parts, so it takes thousands of people to get it ready to launch again after it lands from a previous mission.

The space shuttle's main parts include the orbiter, the solid rocket boosters, and the **external** tank. The orbiter is like an airplane. The solid rocket boosters are the rockets that power the space shuttle during the first part of its journey, and the external tank is a giant fuel tank that supplies fuel to the orbiter's engines.

Orbiter

There are now three working orbiters: *Endeavor*, *Discovery*, and *Atlantis*. The orbiters each consist of a crew cabin, a payload bay, and three space shuttle main engines.

The crew cabin is the front of the orbiter. This is where the astronauts ride. The payload bay is in the middle. It is where experiments, supplies, and equipment for the mission are kept.

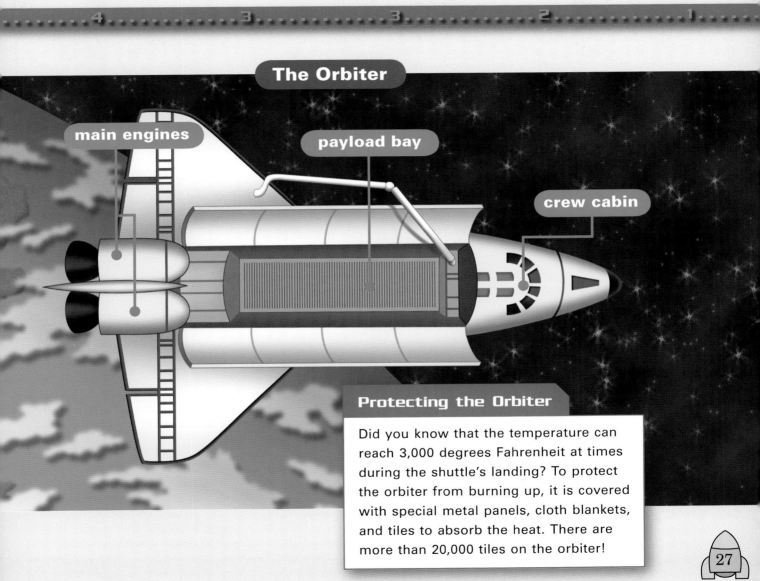

The Orbiter

main engines

payload bay

crew cabin

Protecting the Orbiter

Did you know that the temperature can reach 3,000 degrees Fahrenheit at times during the shuttle's landing? To protect the orbiter from burning up, it is covered with special metal panels, cloth blankets, and tiles to absorb the heat. There are more than 20,000 tiles on the orbiter!

The engines on the orbiter are called the space shuttle main engines. They are 14 feet long, and each one has more than 50,000 parts! For the first two minutes of flight, the space shuttle's rockets make the shuttle fly, but after that, the main engines do all of the work.

Just before the main engines take over, the space shuttle is flying at about 3,000 miles per hour. The main engines are so powerful that they increase the speed of the shuttle to over 17,000 miles per hour in just six minutes! The main engines also use fuel very quickly. In fact, the main engines would drain a family-sized swimming pool in less than 25 seconds!

Solid Rocket Boosters

The solid rocket boosters are the rockets that lift the space shuttle off the ground and power it for the first two minutes of its flight. The two rockets, each over 149 feet tall, are attached to the orbiter, one on each side. Most of the fire and smoke you see during a launch comes from these rockets.

After two minutes, the rockets have used all of their fuel and break away from the orbiter, falling into the ocean to be recovered and used again for another mission.

Solid Rocket Boosters

The solid rocket boosters arrive at the launch pad in pieces and must be put together. They go through a process called "stacking" where the pieces are stacked on top of one another like blocks. This takes about three weeks!

The solid rocket boosters send the shuttle into space.

External Tank

The external tank is the large orange fuel tank on the outside of the orbiter that holds the fuel for the space shuttle's main engines. The orange color comes from the foam that is put on the outside of the tank to keep the fuel inside very cold.

The fuel tank is the only part of the space shuttle that doesn't get used again in other missions. When the shuttle reaches orbit, the engines have used all of the fuel in the tank, so it is released from the orbiter and falls through the atmosphere. Most of the external tank is destroyed as it falls. Whatever is left lands in the ocean.

The external tank sits on the launch pad. Less than ten minutes after the shuttle is launched, the tank will be released and will fall back to Earth.

Once the orbiter is ready to fly, many workers spend months putting the payloads, or the experiments and equipment, together inside the payload bay. Small payloads can be brought on while the orbiter is flat on the ground in the orbiter processing **facility**, a building that is like an enormous garage. However, most of the larger payloads are brought on while the space shuttle is standing up on the launch pad.

The payloads put into the orbiter payload bay on the launch pad include the heaviest payloads and almost all the pieces needed to build the International Space Station. The payloads must pass many tests before they are ready to be brought on board the shuttle. These tests can include equipment and wiring tests. Leaks are checked for, as well.

Once these tests are done, the payloads are placed in a huge structure called the payload canister, which will be sent to the launch pad. Everything inside it will be moved into the space shuttle's payload bay.

The payload bay will be filled with all the experiments and equipment packed on the shuttle.

The payload canister is exactly the same size as the space shuttle's payload bay.

CHAPTER 6

10 . . . . 9 . . . . 8 . . . . 7 . . . . 6 . . . .

On the Launch Pad

All of the space shuttle's pieces are extremely heavy, and they must be put together before the shuttle can be moved to the launch pad. They are **assembled** in a very tall building called the **vehicle** assembly building. Workers use huge cranes that can hold several hundred tons to lift the pieces and put them together.

The space shuttle is assembled in a special building.

A Slow Journey

When the space shuttle is ready and has passed all of its safety tests, it is moved over six miles to the launch pad by a vehicle called a crawler transporter. The crawler is a square vehicle with wheels like those on a bulldozer. The crawler is as heavy as 2,000 cars!

The space shuttle's journey on top of the crawler is very slow. Though the crawler is powerful—it must carry a load weighing 12 million pounds—it moves at only about one mile per hour. That is slower than most people walk! It takes over six hours for the crawler to take the space shuttle to the launch pad.

Weighing over five and a half million pounds, the crawler is the largest land vehicle in the world. For an idea of the crawler's size, look at the man standing at the back right side of the crawler.

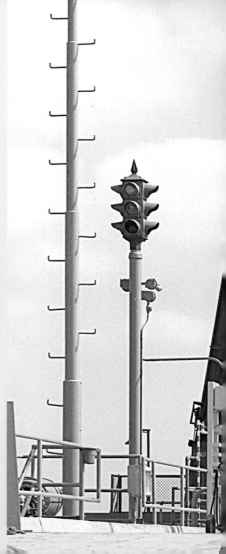

The launch pads used to launch the space shuttles are the same ones that were used to launch the Apollo missions, which took astronauts to the moon. Each pad is a huge octagon that covers a quarter-mile area of land. Each has a towering metal frame called the fixed support structure, which has twenty floors that provide **access** to a shuttle on the pad.

The flat base that the space shuttle stands on is called the **mobile** launch platform. It is actually separate from the launch pad; it is moved with the space shuttle to the launch pad on the crawler. There are also two large tanks on either side of the launch pad. These tanks supply the external tank on the shuttle with the fuel used by the shuttle's main engines.

The space shuttle stands on the launch pad while workers ready it for launching.

Once the space shuttle is delivered to the launch pad, it doesn't get launched right away. It will sit on the launch pad for at least a month before the start of the launch countdown. During this time, the **rotating** service structure moves around the shuttle to protect it from the weather and to allow workers who are preparing the shuttle for flight to get to the shuttle easily.

These workers will run many tests to make sure the space shuttle, its payloads, and the equipment on the launch pad are ready for the launch.

This is also the time when the large payloads are put into the payload bay. The payload canister is brought to the launch pad. Then it is lifted by crane to the part of the rotating service structure called the changeout room. The payloads are then moved from the canister to the payload bay of the shuttle.

The payload canister is raised to the launch pad, where its contents will be placed inside the shuttle's payload bay.

39

Launch Sequence

What most people remember about watching the countdown to a space shuttle launch is the final ten seconds, with that famous phrase, "3 – 2 – 1 . . . **Ignition** . . . Blast-off!" But the countdown actually starts days before those memorable final seconds. Those seconds are only a small, though very exciting, part of the launch sequence. The launch sequence is a schedule that includes all of the steps necessary to make sure the space shuttle and everything needed to launch it are ready to go.

A few days before the scheduled liftoff, the launch team gets a report from weather experts about weather conditions that might affect the launch. Rain, lightning, extreme temperatures, and strong winds can all make launching the space shuttle highly dangerous.

For this reason, there are strict rules about weather at the launch pad. The launch will be postponed if weather conditions are unfavorable in any way or if there is a good chance that conditions will be unfavorable in the few minutes after the launch.

What Those Letters Mean

During a countdown, when people say, "L minus three" or "T minus five," they are describing a particular moment during that launch sequence. *L* stands for *launch*, while *T* stands for *time*. For example, three days before the launch date is "L minus three days," written as "L–3 days." When the day of the launch arrives, the moments are referred to as *T* instead of *L*. Thus, seven minutes and thirty seconds before launch is "T minus seven minutes, thirty seconds" or "T–7 minutes, 30 seconds."

This launch had to be delayed because of bad weather.

LAUNCH SEQUENCE

The launch sequence in place is followed exactly for each launch. The sequence can be stopped at any time if there is a problem.

L–3 days
- Space suits are packed into the shuttle.
- The crew cabin is checked.

L–2 days
- Fuel for the external tank is pumped into storage tanks on either side of the launch pad.
- Controls and switches in the crew cabin are checked.

L–1 day
- The rotating service structure around the shuttle is moved away.

Launch day
- The external tank is filled with fuel, a process that takes several hours.

The countdown until the space shuttle launches has begun.

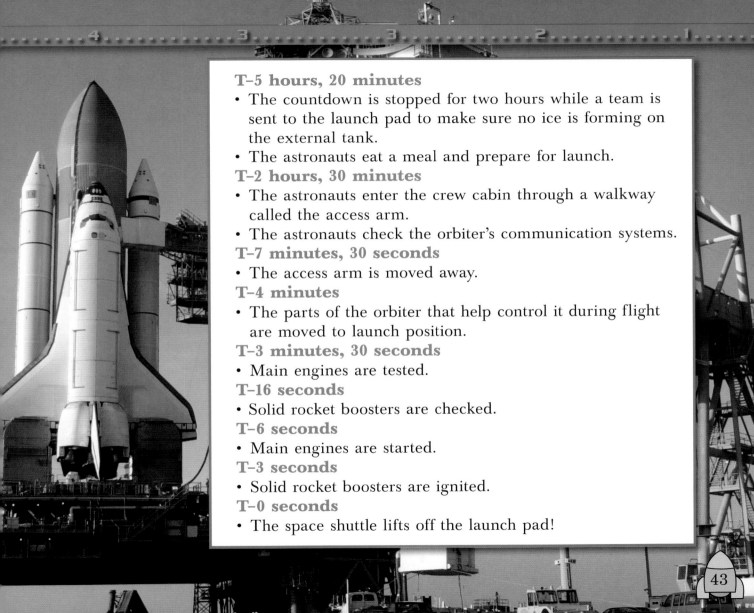

T–5 hours, 20 minutes
- The countdown is stopped for two hours while a team is sent to the launch pad to make sure no ice is forming on the external tank.
- The astronauts eat a meal and prepare for launch.

T–2 hours, 30 minutes
- The astronauts enter the crew cabin through a walkway called the access arm.
- The astronauts check the orbiter's communication systems.

T–7 minutes, 30 seconds
- The access arm is moved away.

T–4 minutes
- The parts of the orbiter that help control it during flight are moved to launch position.

T–3 minutes, 30 seconds
- Main engines are tested.

T–16 seconds
- Solid rocket boosters are checked.

T–6 seconds
- Main engines are started.

T–3 seconds
- Solid rocket boosters are ignited.

T–0 seconds
- The space shuttle lifts off the launch pad!

Two minutes after liftoff, when the space shuttle is already 30 miles from the ground, the solid rocket boosters separate from the shuttle and tumble into the ocean. Parachutes slow the boosters' fall and keep them from being destroyed when they hit the water.

Once the space shuttle reaches orbit, about 8½ minutes after liftoff, the external tank is released from the orbiter. The space shuttle is now orbiting Earth, and the astronauts are ready to begin their mission in space! The huge doors of the payload bay are opened, and the events planned so carefully by mission planners begin.

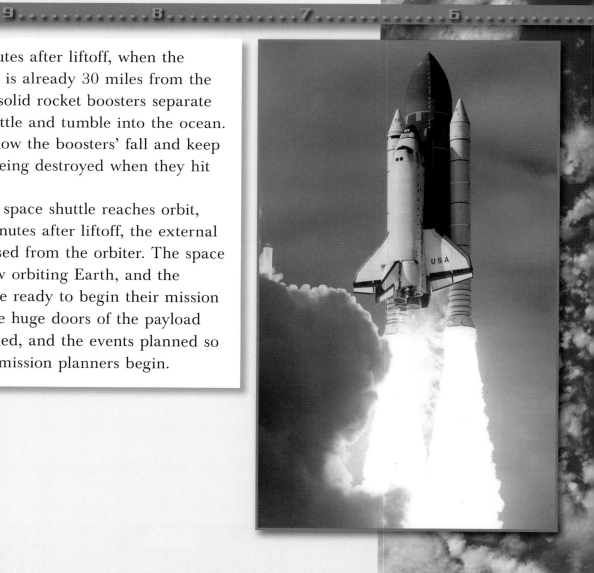

The shuttle is now in orbit.

The Next Mission

At the same time space shuttle program workers are celebrating a successful launch, they're getting ready for the next one. While the astronauts are in orbit, back on Earth two ships called the *Liberty Star* and the *Freedom Star* are searching for the solid rocket boosters that landed in the ocean after separating from the shuttle.

When the orbiter itself lands safely after a mission, it is on the runway for only a few hours before it is taken into the orbiter processing facility to get it ready for the next flight.

Divers put a plug into the bottom of the booster. Then air is pumped into it. This pushes the water out and makes the booster float straight up until it falls over. The booster is connected to the ship and towed to land, where it will be dried, cleaned, and prepared for another launch.

Platforms are placed all around the orbiter so workers can reach every part of it. Then work begins on the payload bay, main engines, and tiles. The tools and payloads that were brought back at the end of the mission are removed from the payload bay. Workers then prepare the bay for whatever will be included on the next mission.

The space shuttle main engines are removed, looked over, and tested after every flight. The tiles and metal panels that protect the orbiter from the extreme heat of re-entering the atmosphere are also looked over to make sure there is no damage.

Workers will spend many months carefully preparing the space shuttle for its next flight.

These workers are examining the shuttle for signs of problems.

Exploring the Rest of Our Solar System

Exploring space is not only exciting, but very important. Much has been learned from the work that is done aboard the space shuttle and Space Station. In addition to learning about our planet, we also learn about the other planets that orbit the Sun in our solar system, the Milky Way.

Though some of the eight planets share a few of the same characteristics, each planet in our solar system is unique.

Some planets are rocky, covered with mountains, volcanoes, and valleys, while others are made of gases and have no solid core or crust. Each planet's size, weight, and climate are very different.

The space shuttle and the Space Station are not the only spacecrafts gathering information about our solar system. Other spacecraft, ones that do not carry astronauts, are currently in space, increasing our knowledge of the solar system.

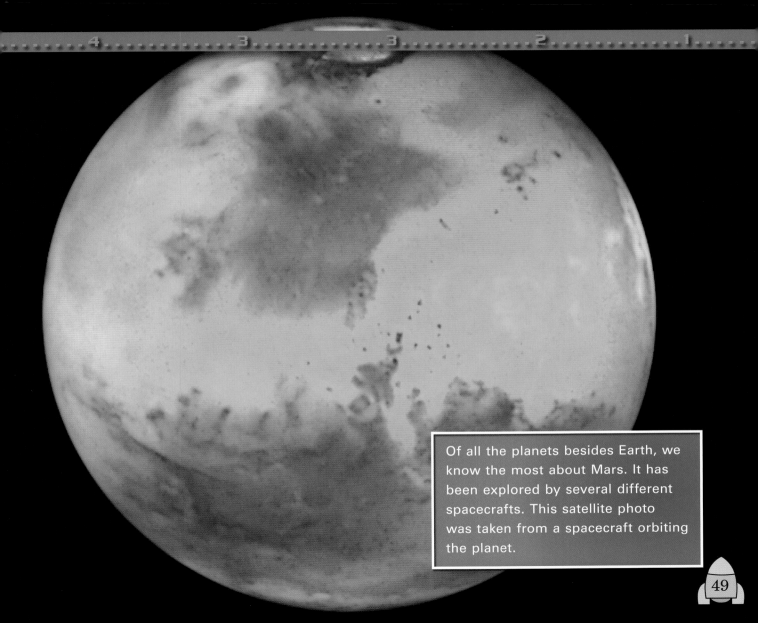

Of all the planets besides Earth, we know the most about Mars. It has been explored by several different spacecrafts. This satellite photo was taken from a spacecraft orbiting the planet.

Mars Spacecraft

The Mars exploration rovers, *Spirit* and *Opportunity*, are twin spacecraft that landed on opposite sides of the planet. Their mission is to travel the planet to give scientists a better idea about Mars's surface. These rovers are on the surface of Mars right now! They are using many tools, including cameras and even magnets that collect rock particles.

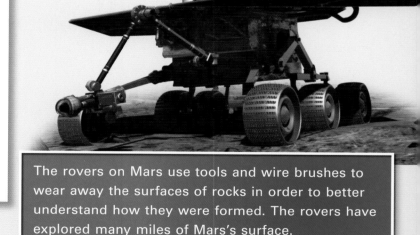

The rovers on Mars use tools and wire brushes to wear away the surfaces of rocks in order to better understand how they were formed. The rovers have explored many miles of Mars's surface.

This is a view of the sunset on Mars from one of the rovers.

Saturn Spacecraft

A spacecraft called *Cassini-Huygens* was launched a few years ago to explore Saturn. It was the first spacecraft to explore Saturn, a planet with thousands of vivid rings and at least 47 moons. The spacecraft is still giving us details about the planet today.

The part of the spacecraft called *Cassini* orbits Saturn and records information about the planet. *Cassini* released a second, smaller spacecraft called *Huygens* to land on the surface of Saturn's largest moon, Titan.

The spacecraft *Cassini* took this photo of one of Saturn's moons. Saturn is in the background.

51

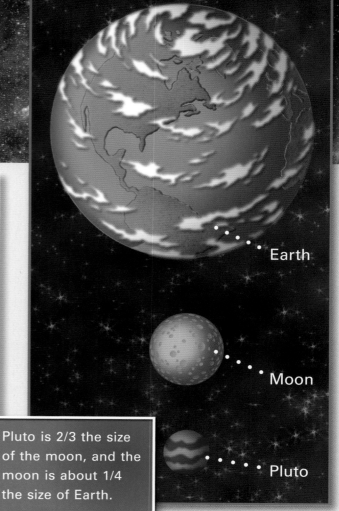

Pluto Spacecraft

For most of the past century, Pluto was considered to be our most distant planet. On August 24, 2006, however, a group of astronomers and scientists decided that Pluto should not be classified as a planet.

A new spacecraft, *New Horizons,* was just launched into space, carrying cameras and other tools. It will take almost ten years to reach Pluto. Once it arrives, many of our questions about Pluto's atmosphere, surface, and climate may be answered.

Pluto is 2/3 the size of the moon, and the moon is about 1/4 the size of Earth.

Earth

Moon

Pluto

The Future of Space Exploration

The things we achieve in space and the amazing places we go in the future depend on the success of the missions happening today. The research done on the space shuttle and the International Space Station must be successful in order for us to learn what we need to know about how spending long amounts of time in space affects the human body.

Spacecraft sent to other planets must help us learn as much as possible before we can think of sending people to distant planets. A key goal for exploring space in the future is sending astronauts to Mars, and with the help of these programs, we're right on track. In fact, maybe you could be the first astronaut to step on Mars!

This photograph of the Milky Way Galaxy was taken from a huge space telescope.

53

access a way of approaching something

assembled put together

bay a place where cargo is stored

buoyancy the ability to float

coordinator someone who makes sure things are going well

docking joining up with another space shuttle or a Space Station

engineer someone who uses science to solve problems

external outside

facility a building that serves a particular purpose

ignition the act of starting an engine

mobile able to move

monitor observe

nutritionist someone who studies how to have a balanced, healthy diet

payload any equipment, experiments, or supplies aboard the space shuttle

rotating to turn around

simulator something that imitates something else

specialist a person who has unique knowledge about something

vehicle something that transports people or things

weightlessness when in space, the feeling of having no weight due to a lack of gravity